First 1000
Words

HINKLER
BOOKS

Julie Haydon

First published in 2006
by Hinkler Books Pty Ltd
45–55 Fairchild Street
Heatherton Victoria 3202 Australia
www.hinklerbooks.com

© Hinkler Books Pty Ltd 2006

10 9 8
11 10

Internal Design: Ivan Finnegan
Cover Design: Hinkler Design Studio
Photography: Peter Wakeman
Prepress: Graphic Print Group

ISBN : 978 1 7415 7953 6

Printed and bound in China

CONTENTS

THE
Face

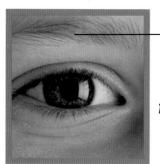

eyebrow

eye

eyelid

eyelashes

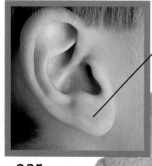

ear

earlobe

hair

forehead

mouth

lip

A HAPPY FACE

4

nostril *nose* *tongue* *teeth*

tasting

seeing

touching

smelling

hearing

cheek

chin

5

THE
Body

head

shoulder

neck

arm

chest

abdomen

finger

wrist

waist

hip

hand

6

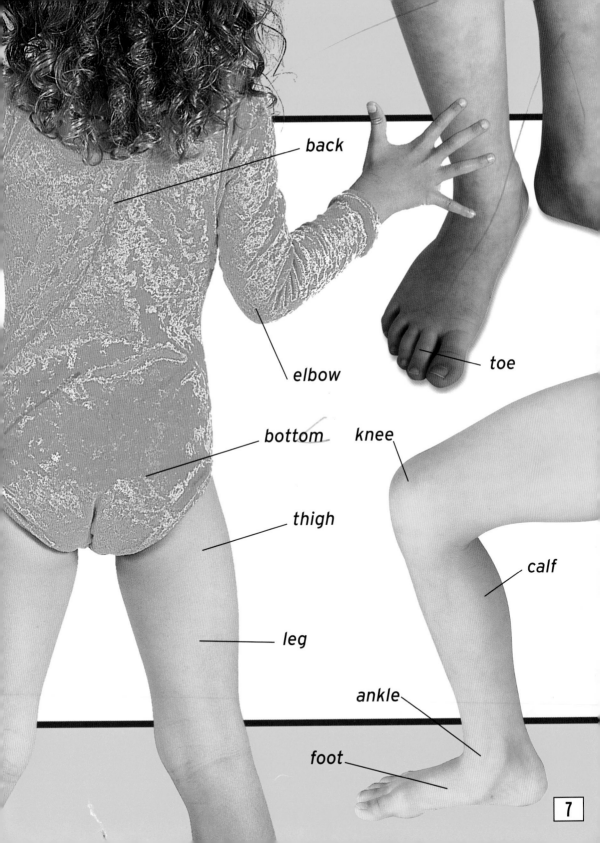

back

elbow

toe

bottom   knee

thigh

calf

leg

ankle

foot

7

MY
Family

my birth certificate

CERTIFICATE OF BIRTH

my brother

my pa

my kitten

my nana

my twin

ME

8

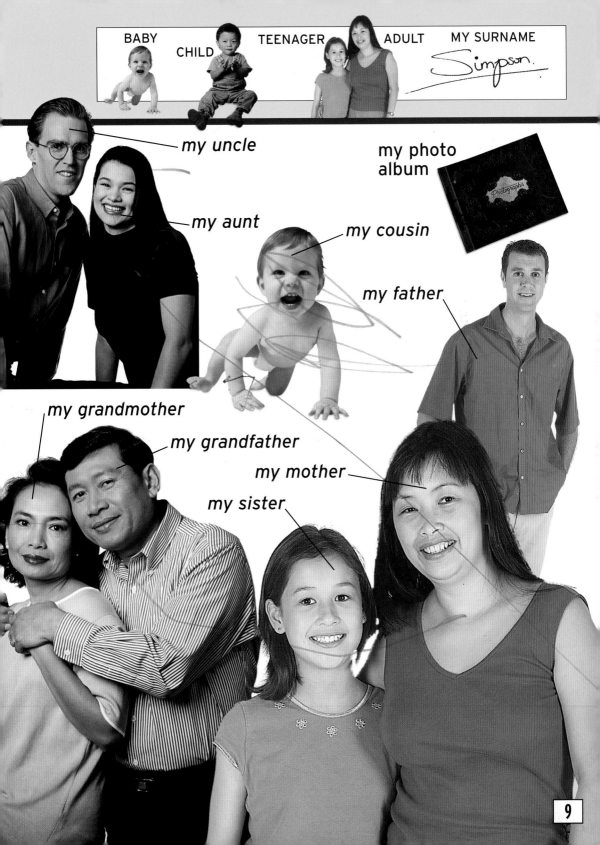

BABY
CHILD
TEENAGER
ADULT
MY SURNAME
Simpson.

my uncle

my photo
album

my aunt

my cousin

my father

my grandmother

my grandfather

my mother

my sister

9

BABY'S Things

bootees

blanket

pins

high chair

rattle

potty

cotton balls

soft toy

monitors

BIB

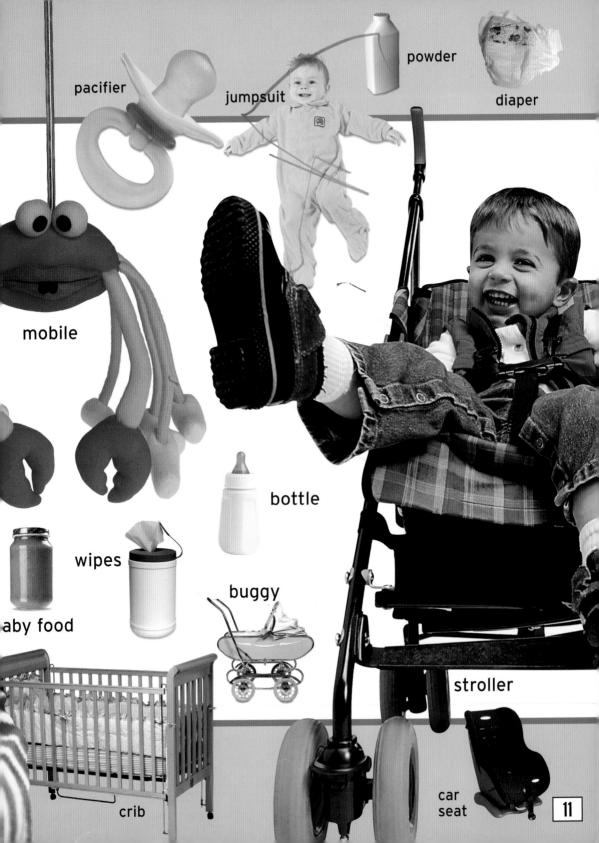

pacifier

jumpsuit

powder

diaper

mobile

bottle

wipes

aby food

buggy

stroller

crib

car
seat

11

Clothes

tights

shorts

sweater

overalls

jeans

tank top

BOOTS

coat

tie

trousers

shoes

underpants

shirt

leotard

dress

T-shirt

skirt

socks

underpants

jacket

sneakers

13

Accessories

satchel

hat

hairclip

key ring

beret

braces

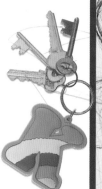

EARRING

headband

ribbons

necklace

scrunchies

backpack

handbag

evening bag

gloves

belt

watch

cap

rings

fake tattoo

bracelets

15

Food

egg

sandwich

sugar

butter

cereal

juice

yogurt

bread

FISH

granola bars

crackers

hot chocolate

oatmeal

milk

cheese

meat

rice

pasta

honey

salad

17

PARTY
Food

muffin

fruit tart

potato
chips

pretzels

JELLYBEANS

lollipop

donut

popcorn

jello

cookies

18

nuts

candy
cane

marshmallows

cake

chocolate

soda

pizza

hamburger

fries

19

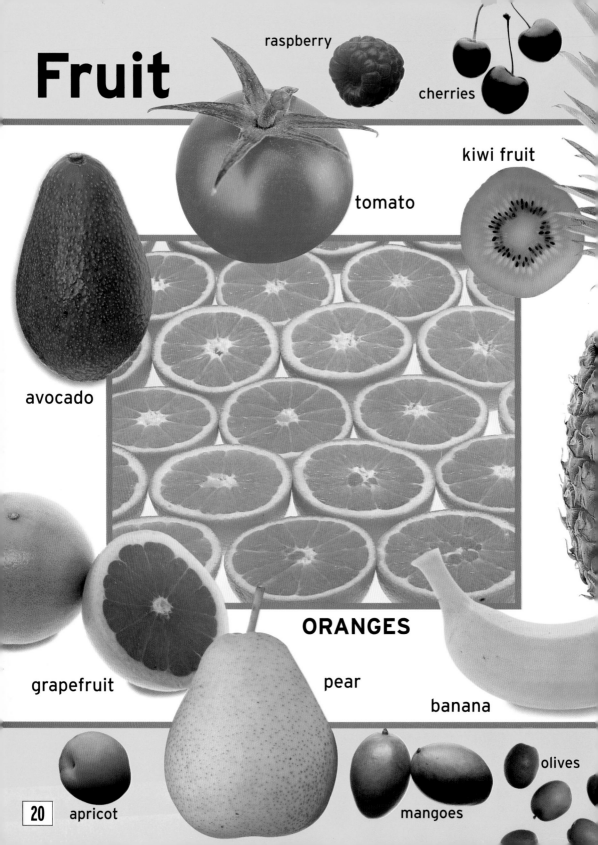

Fruit

raspberry

cherries

kiwi fruit

tomato

avocado

ORANGES

grapefruit

pear

banana

apricot

mangoes

olives

mandarin
orange

dates

strawberry

apple

pineapple

lemon

watermelon

grapes

peaches

Vegetables

asparagus

onion

cabbages

leeks

carrots

SWEET CORN

cauliflower

radish

spinach

mushrooms

rhubarb

22

broccoli

zucchini

parsnip

beet

lettuce

green
onions

turnip

potatoes

eggplant

peas

Plants

acorns

fern

grass

holly

ivy

cactus

LEAVES

blossom

seedling

pine cone

moss

trunk

bark

bottlebrush

wattle

gum flowers

palm tree

weeping willow

oak leaves

maple

flytrap

potted plants

Flowers

pansy

violet

bouquet

daisy

chrysanthemum

orchid

bluebell

SUNFLOWER

tulip

cornflower

knotweed

gardenia

zinnia

carnation

hibiscus

marigold

ris

rose

lily

freesia

gerbera

Gardening

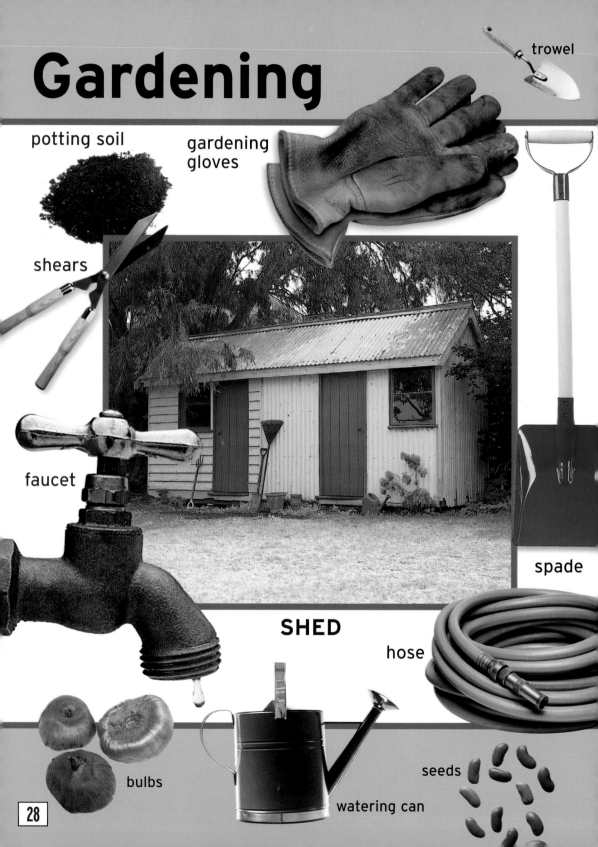

trowel

potting soil

gardening gloves

shears

faucet

SHED

spade

hose

bulbs

watering can

seeds

28

compost bin

flowerpots

clippers

gardening hat

wheelbarrow

shovel

lawnmower

weeds

rake

rock

29

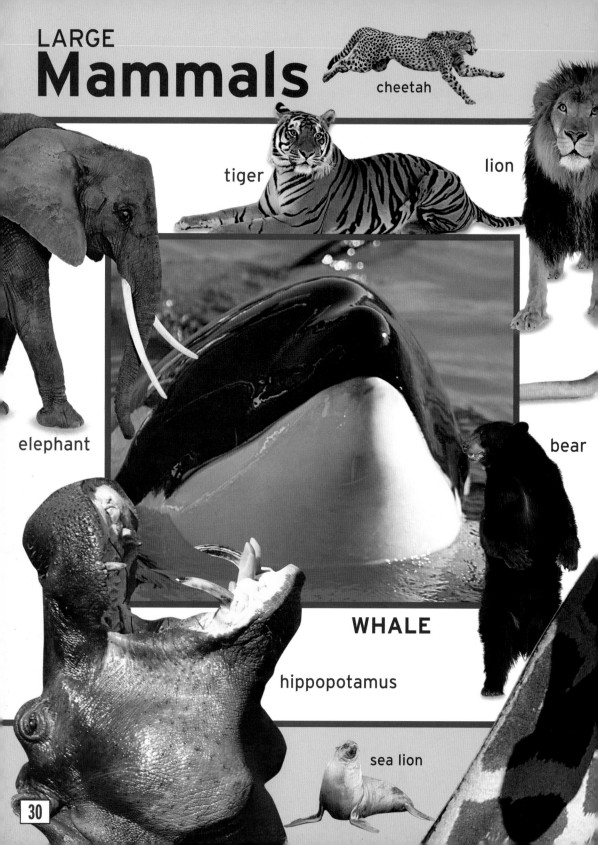

LARGE
Mammals

cheetah

tiger

lion

elephant

WHALE

bear

hippopotamus

sea lion

rhinoceros

polar bear

deer

monkey

dolphins

kangaroo

camel

leopard

giraffe

chimpanzee

puma

gorilla

moose

SMALL
Mammals

hedgehog

rat

squirrel

otter

raccoon

meerkats

BADGER

koala

opossum

fox

echidna

skunk

wombat

chipmunk

hare

possum

wolverine

bat

beaver

Tasmanian devil

armadillo

Birds

emu

pigeon

owl

kingfisher

puffin

parrot

eagle

ALBATROSS

pelican

ostrich

macaw

falcon

hawk

peacock

lovebird

flamingo

crane

toucan

swans

vulture

woodpecker

REPTILES AND
Amphibians

bullfrog

alligator

skink

iguana

gecko

KOMODO DRAGON

cobra

terrapin

tortoise

toad

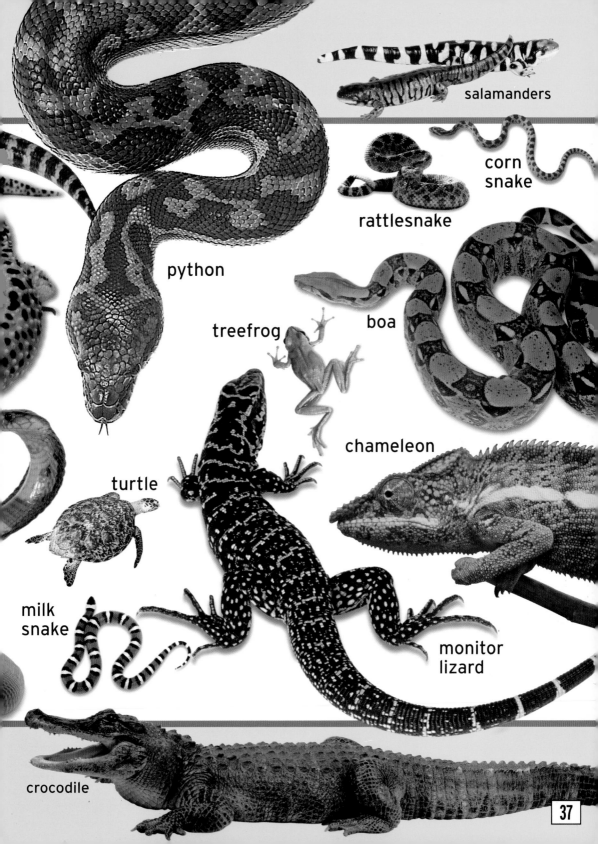

salamanders

corn snake

rattlesnake

python

boa

treefrog

chameleon

turtle

milk snake

monitor lizard

crocodile

WATER
Animals

puffer fish

lobster

herrings

tuna

oysters

shrimp

JELLYFISH

angelfish

stingray

seadragon

coral

shark

damsel fish

cod

sardines

salmon

sea horse

starfish

catfish

crab

eel

pike

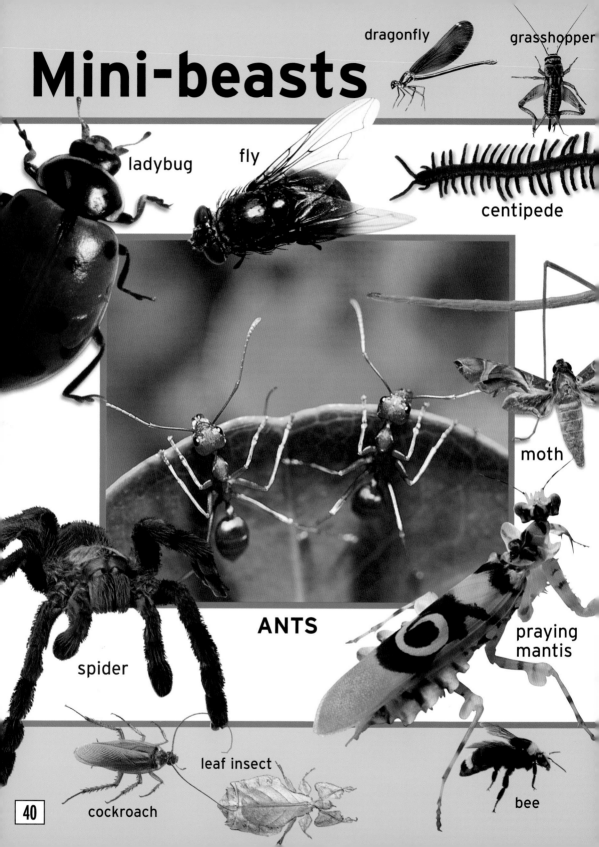

Mini-beasts

dragonfly

grasshopper

ladybug

fly

centipede

moth

ANTS

spider

praying
mantis

leaf insect

cockroach

bee

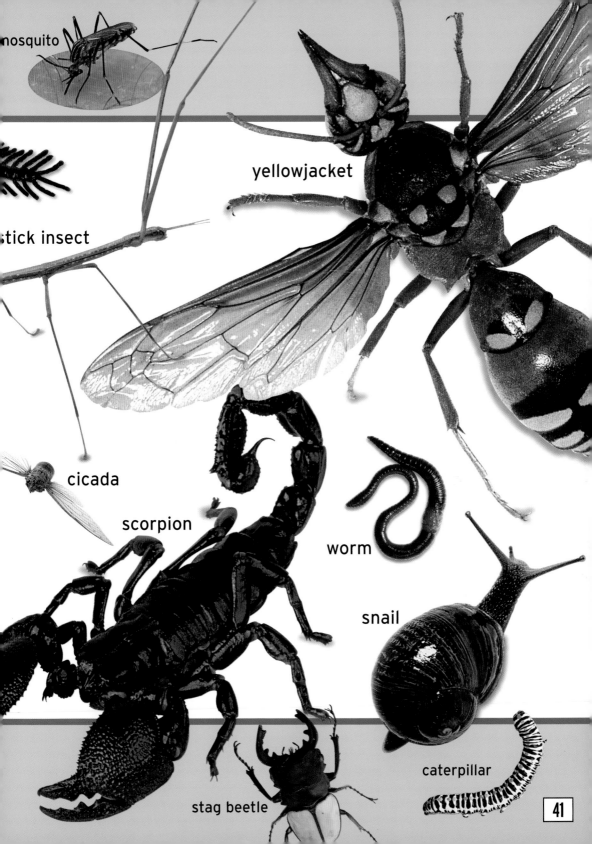

mosquito

yellowjacket

stick insect

cicada

scorpion

worm

snail

stag beetle

caterpillar

ANIMAL
Bodies

hoof

feathers

horn

wings

tail

FANGS

fur

spines

talons

whiskers

scales

paw

claws

gill

mane

snout

antlers

pouch

tusks

beak

fin

43

Pets

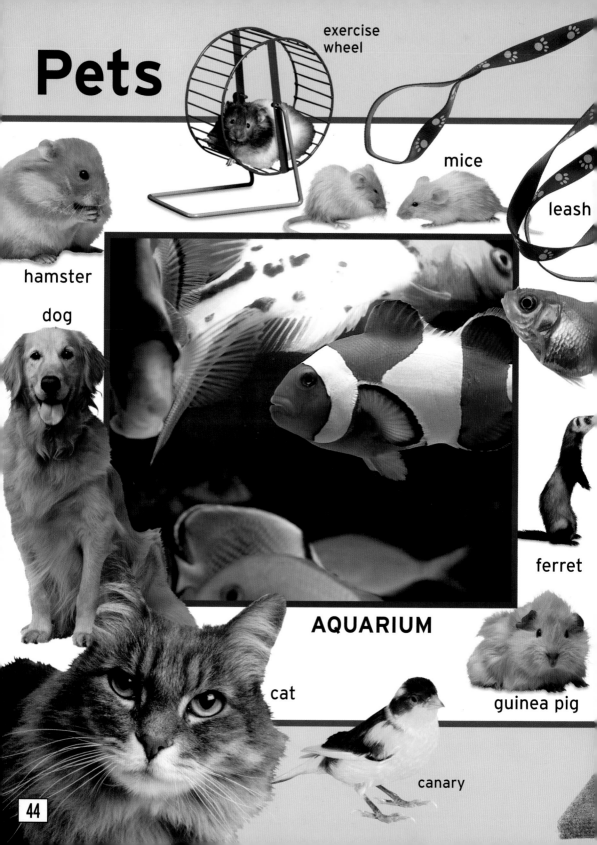

exercise wheel

mice

leash

hamster

dog

AQUARIUM

ferret

cat

guinea pig

canary

pony

doghouse

collar

pet toy

rabbit

goldfish

cage

stable

scratching post

saddle

pet bed

45

A House

door knocker

mailbox

balcony

window

curtain

lawn

doormat

lock

wall

blind

door

porch

bricks

gutter

fence

garage

drive

roof

trash
can

doorknob

IN THE
Bedroom

dresser

night-light

photo frame

quilt   *pillow*

alarm
clock

toy box

BED

trophy

books

bathrobe   wardrobe

slippers

rocking horse

pajamas

mattress

hat rack

teddy bear

rug

poster

49

IN THE
Bathroom

toilet

hairbrush

rubber duck

shampoo

washcloth

WASHBASIN

plug

make-up

medicine

comb

tissues

toothpaste

toilet paper

airdryer

shower

mirror

towel

bathtub

toothbrush

soap

bubble bath

51

video recorder

coffee table

remote control

lamp

rocking chair

cushion

BOOKSHELF

vase

television

compact disc

video cassettes

picture

carpet

beanbag

games table

coasters

headphones

couch

newspaper

stereo

magazines

53

IN THE
Kitchen

juicer

kitchen
scales

range

electric
mixer

cooktop

toaster

apron

BENCHTOP

refrigerator

stool

food
processor

table

cutting board

chair

breadmaker

kettle

jar

cookbook

sink

dishwasher

microwave oven

IN THE
Cabinet

bowl

saucepan

cake pan

plate

dishwashing liquid

PLATTER

sponge

teapot

cup

dishtowel

rubber gloves

wooden
spoon

rolling pin

glass

knife

fork

spoon

tray

egg beater

fry pan

jug

57

IN THE
Study

envelope

desk

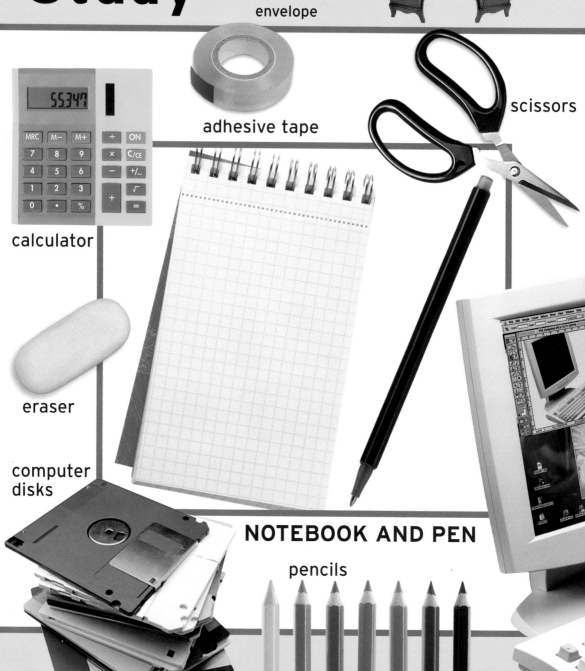

adhesive tape

scissors

55347

calculator

eraser

computer
disks

NOTEBOOK AND PEN

pencils

dictionary

stapler

telephone

diary

office chair

paper clip

sharpener

paper

computer

ruler

glue

CRAFT PASTE

ALL NATURAL

59

HOUSEHOLD Items

nails

pliers

screw

ax

clothes hanger

power socket

WASHING MACHINE

vacuum cleaner

saw

hammer

wrench

tape measure

paintbrush

screwdrivers

iron

dryer

ladder

ironing board

tool kit

paint can

electric drill

Birthday Party

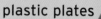
plastic plates

candy

banne[r]

greeting
card

plastic
cup

BIRTHDAY CAKE wrapping paper

gifts

candles

gift bag

62

streamers

fruit drink

bow

party whistles

invitation

BIRTHDAY

straws

badge

party hat

birthday girl

7 today

friends

mask

party game

63

Fancy Dress

wand

bumblebee

glitter

Little Bo Peep

king

butterfly

mouse

octopus

flower

64

kitty

tiara

fairy wings

sea lion

costume

bunny

starfish

puppy

calf

pirate

wig

clown

Toys

dice

dollhouse

dinosaur

wagon

soldier

dragon

PUZZLE

blackboard

cowboy

checkerboard

cube

skipping rope

doll

cards

spaceship

robot

tricycle

blocks

slinky

dominoes

marbles

67

FAVORITE Things

jewelry

kite

boomerang

money

crayon

piggy bank

penguin

SEE-SAW

telescope

ukulele

stickers

scarf

magnet

quilt

fishing rod

chess set

coconut

tutu

radio

Frisbee

yo-yo

69

SPORTS
Equipment

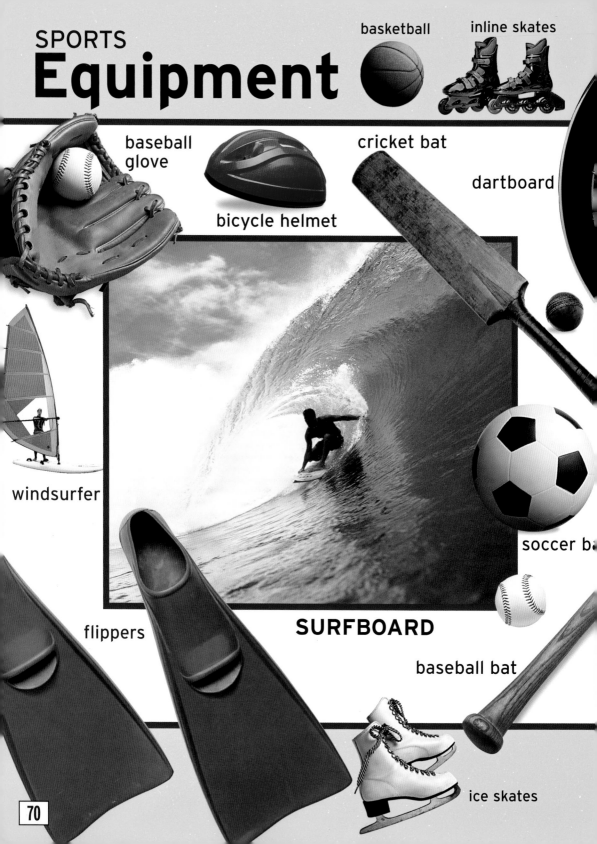

basketball

inline skates

baseball glove

bicycle helmet

cricket bat

dartboard

windsurfer

soccer ba

flippers

SURFBOARD

baseball bat

ice skates

whistle

skis

darts

stopwatch

30
28
26
24
22
20
18
16
58
56
54
52
50
48
46
12
15
9
6
1/10

bicycle

goggles

wetsuit

tennis racket

football

field hockey
stick

71

MUSICAL
Instruments

bells

flute

clarinet

triang[le]

harp

ACOUSTIC GUITAR

cello

maracas

xylophone

piano

recorder

accordion

banjo

tambourine

trumpet

cymbals

saxophone

bagpipes

drums

electric guitar

violin

73

ON THE
Farm

scarecrow

horse

foal

hen

chick

pig

donkey

duck

SHEEPDOG

lamb

rooster

tractor

cow

farmer

farmhouse

goats

sheep

field

goose

hay bale

gate

75

AT THE
Beach

ice cream

beach ball

deckchair

seaweed

sunscreen

ROCK POOL

swim ring

shells

sea

bucket
and
spade

sandcastle

beach
umbrella

sand

seagull

sailboat

swimsuit

sunhat

drink

sandals

basket

sunglasses

Camping

hiking boot

sleeping mat

trail mix

Swiss army knife

binoculars

thermos

gas lam

MAP

camping stove

compass

matches

rope

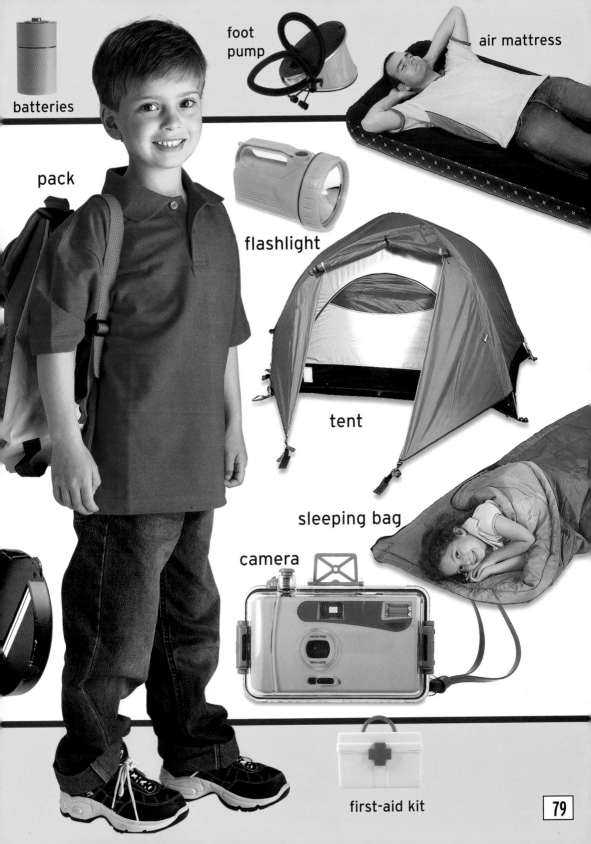

batteries

foot pump

air mattress

pack

flashlight

tent

sleeping bag

camera

first-aid kit

79

Transport

helicopter

bus

ambulance

cab

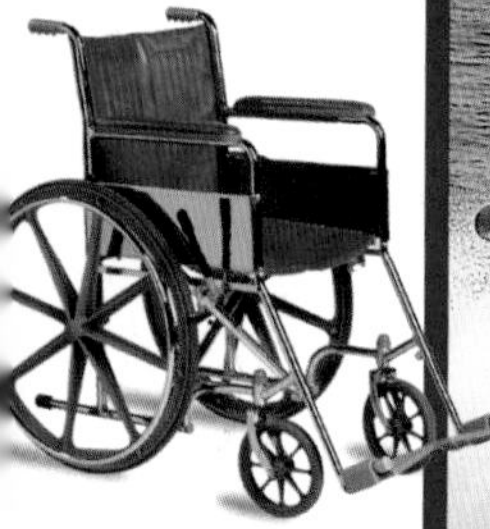

wheelchair

BOAT

motorcycle

fire engine

scooter

jet ski

car

ship

airplane

skateboard

truck

yacht

hot-air balloon

racing car

submarine

train

PEOPLE
at Work

electrician

chef

sailor

ballerina

doctor

scientist

FIREFIGHTERS

artist

decorator

detective

judge

soccer player

plumber

police officer

boxer

waiter

astronaut

builder

nurse

office worker

teacher

Actions

talking

climbing

drawing

hugging

sitting

HIDING

crying

reading

84

drinking

running

sleeping

playing

cutting

eating

kicking

frowning

jumping

reaching

writing

laughing

Opposites

open

closed

fat

dry

thin

wet

over

under

push

pull

down

up

young

old

short

long

empty

full

big

clean

small

dirty

Numbers

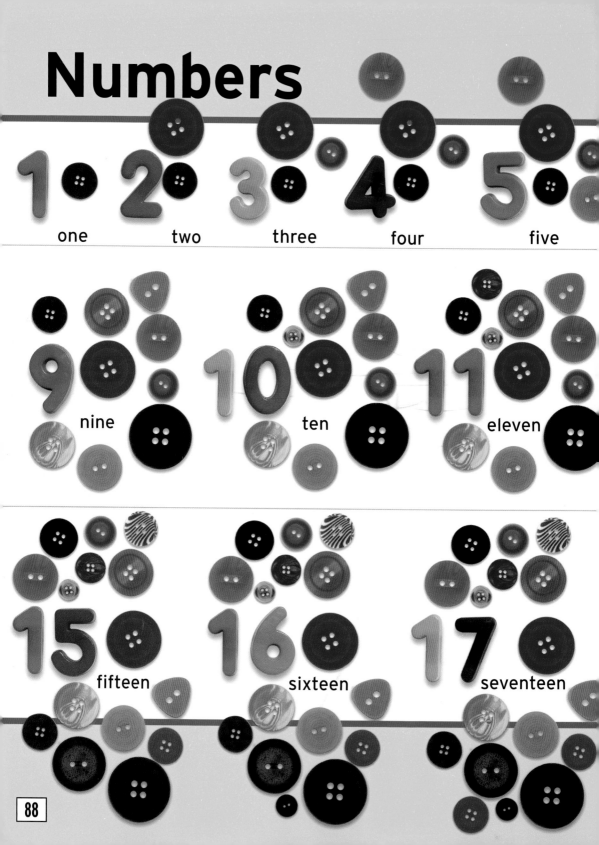

1 one

2 two

3 three

4 four

5 five

9 nine

10 ten

11 eleven

15 fifteen

16 sixteen

17 seventeen

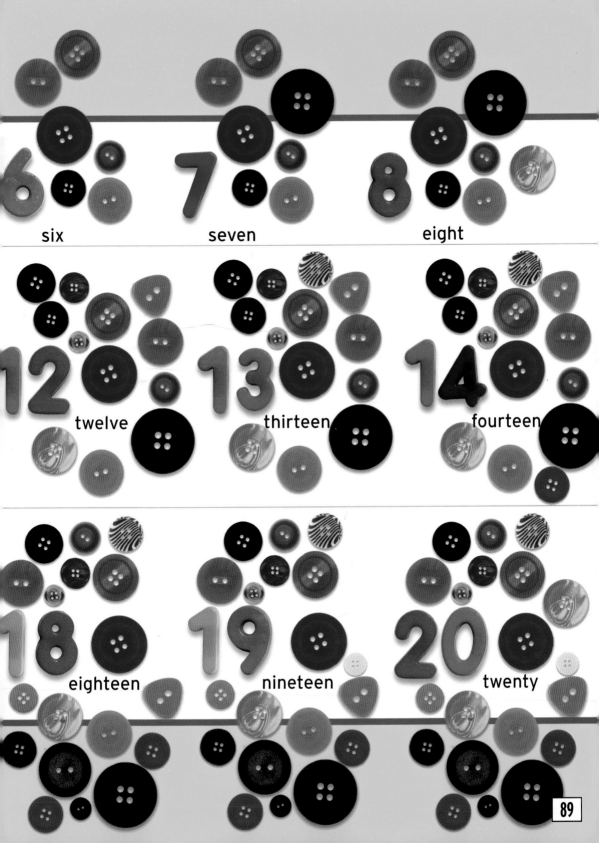

6 six

7 seven

8 eight

12 twelve

13 thirteen

14 fourteen

18 eighteen

19 nineteen

20 twenty

COLORS
and Shapes

yellow

blue

green

gray

orange

purple

white

red

black

brown

pink

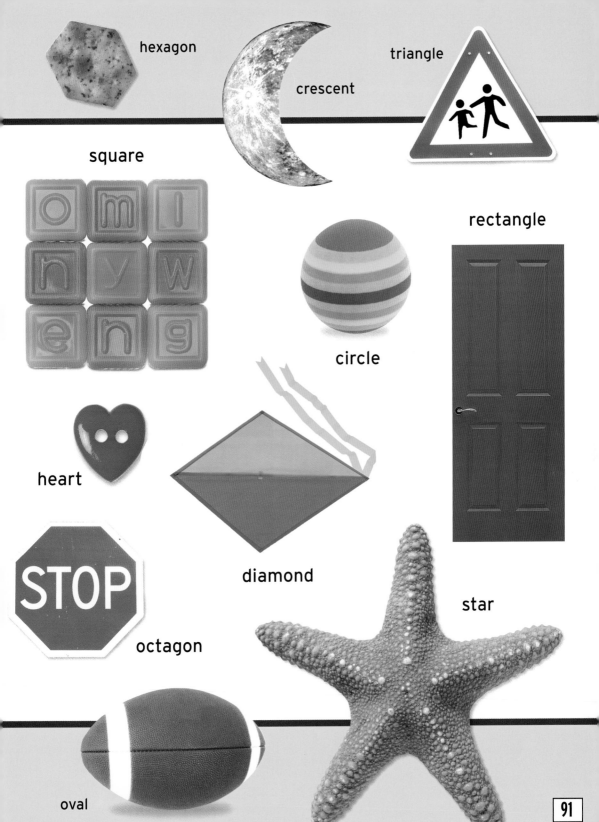

hexagon

crescent

triangle

square

rectangle

circle

heart

diamond

STOP

octagon

star

oval

91

Flags

Belgium

Mexico

Philippines

Australia

Singapore

Hungary

The Czech Republic

Norway

Poland

South Korea

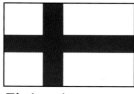
Finland

United Kingdom

Egypt

Brazil

South Africa

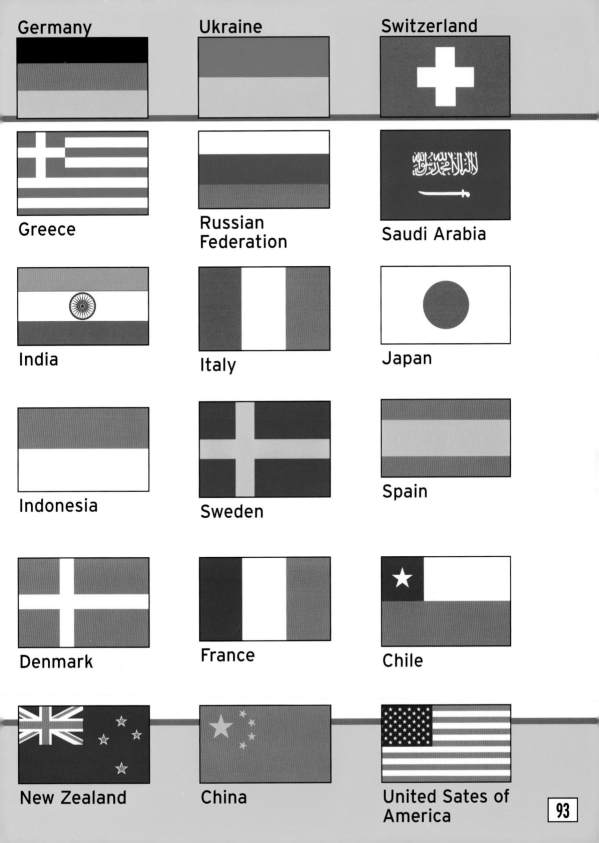

Germany

Ukraine

Switzerland

Greece

Russian
Federation

Saudi Arabia

India

Italy

Japan

Indonesia

Sweden

Spain

Denmark

France

Chile

New Zealand

China

United Sates of
America

93

THE Earth and Sky

clouds

Earth

forest

MOUNTAIN

wind

lightning

desert

eclipse

rain

iceberg

river

moon

pond

rainbow

stars

storm

sun

volcano

cave

waterfall

pasture

95